MW01165914

Poplandia

Andre F. Peltier

abuddhapress@yahoo.com

ISBN: 9798832377407

Alien Buddha Press 2022

®™©

Andre F. Peltier 2022

Avalon—
I'm not drawing a
picture, but only
because I can't think
of anything to draw

The Love Theme from *Switchblade Sisters*

With knives & attitude,
they walk the halls
& sneer
at teachers
& classmates
& children at play.
With empty eyes
in vacant sockets,
they fill the midnight
screens.
My popcorn fingers
slip through
condensation on my Coke
as they sit
in police station
satori.
Lace&Maggie,
Patch&Crabs:
manifestations of
anger.

The girls (w/ their
shock therapy
& their
Frankenstein bolts)
they rained wrath
upon the streets of LA
& the streets of
the world.
"Everybody's gotta be
in a gang,"
they sang.
& the bells
of the Basilica of St.

Cecilia rang
over the Tarn
& through
the land
of Toulouse-Lautrec.

With knives and attitude,
they faced down
Viet Nam
civil war
Watergate America
& saw in the
headlights
of a thousand
Fleetwoods,
the land of a
thousand dances.
Never did
Lace&Maggie
salute the galaxy.
Patch&Crabs
never stood
hand on heart
for the electro-static hum
of the big
bang.

Lock up your sons,
mother,
the jezebels are
coming
for us all, ha ha.
Get to fallout
Shelter security,
The jezebels are
Coming to take us

away, ha ha.
As the lecherous warden
sits in silence,
aloof and alone,
the jezebels
rebrand & rewrite
their Dadaist daydreams
as rational
mathematics.
In the balcony of night,
we sit alone
in aisle-light
satori.

Miyagi's Wisdom and the Lunch-Table Debates
"If do right, no can defense" [1]

When Daniel-san flew,
he caught Johnny in the jaw.
When Daniel-san flew,
he left with the All Valley
Under 18 Karate Tournament
Trophy.
Johnny could no defense.
Johnny learned second place
was no place.
Johnny's glory days
behind him.

We raised glasses
of Faygo Old Fashioned Root Beer,
we filled faces
with Jays Potato Chips,
we took notes with
Jays Potato Chip pencils.
We too would fly
like Daniel-san.
"Kaia, kaia, kaia!"
We too would raise high
our trophies -
our youthful
souls.

Then in Okinawa,
Chozen Toguchi knew the way.
He defensed.
Chozen Toguchi blocked
the sacred Crane.
Shocking - all too shocking.
Had we been lied to?

Could Miyagi-san have been
so wrong?
What were we to make of his
misfortune?
If not for Drum Technique,
Daniel-san would have perished.
If not for the O'Bon festival's
roaring crowd,
Daniel-san would be no more.
We ate and argued.
The Master was misinformed,
and we never looked back.
Like Johnny's,
our glory-days
in the rear view
mirror.

1. *The Karate Kid.* Written by Robert Mark Kamen. Directed by John
   G. Aveldsen. Performance by Noriyuki "Pat" Morita.
   Columbia Pictures, 1984.

9

6: Carbon; C^1

When the crooks tried
to pin the heist on
Superman,
when they made him
look a fool
in front of that sickly child,
he needed a plan.
The weight of his beloved
Krypton
pressed hard upon
his shoulders.
He directed those
incalculable tons of
pressure towards
his cause.
His plan to return
certainty to the poor
boy's heart.
His plan to bring those
villains to justice.
His hands duplicated
the work of eons.
His steel biceps worked
to fuse the opaque carbon.
When he opened his fist,
the translucent perfections
were waiting.
The translucent crystal
gleamed in his palm.
With the glittering diamond,
his plan was set in motion.

1. This poem interpolates a passage from *Action Comics* #115 by
    Schwartz, Yarbrough, and Kaye published by DC Comics in 1947.

Uber Through the Sands of Arrakis

I check my messages
& see I have another
fare.
This Uber side-hustle
is rough,
but it pays the child-support.
This side-hustle puts
food on the table
& keeps the heat on
in winter.
It turns out that between
spice-heads
& the alcohol usage in
The House Atreides,
I've been pretty busy.
Three in the morning
& that punk Paul
is texting me again,
"Hey dude,
I need a lift home.
I had three too many,
hahaha."

What a douchebag!
His frat-boy friends
help him up on top
& away we go.
Through the sands of Arrakis,
I hump those sorry sacks
home again, home again,
home again.

Through the sands of Arrakis,
I travel blind
& forgotten.

11

Graceland

South from Dongola,
we drove through the sunset
and fireworks
to the dawn of
rock and roll.
North from Tupelo,
he road in on the
wings of angels
while seraphim sang,
"Son, that girl
you're foolin' with,
she ain't no good for you."

Memphis at dawn,
crossing the river
and crossing the line.
Hernando de Soto
slept here
and died here
on the banks.
Down in the Delta,
de Soto,
Castilian giant of a man,
died and was buried
among the reeds
and the crocodiles.

Memphis, too,
has buried kings.
North from Tupelo,
he took care of business.
We wandered the ground,
saw the gaudy
Christmas tree

and the maize and blue
television room.
We toured the *Lisa Marie*
and the racquetball court.
We passed the bar
to get to the racquetball court.
In the garden,
a young woman
wept at his grave.
Elvis was long dead
by the time she was born,
but she wept.
Perhaps she listened
to his old records with
her grandfather.
"Blue Moon of Kentucky,"
"Brown Eyed Handsome Man,"
"Blue Suede Shoes."
Perhaps they listened
while she sat on his lap.
He smoked his cigarettes
and bobbed his head
while she stared into his eyes
and loved him.
He made her peanut butter
and banana sandwiches
as they listened to
"Heartbreak Hotel"
and worked in the garden.
He smelled of
aftershave and Beeman's.
She rolled with laughter
as he tried to emulate
the great hip-shake
to the sounds of
"Hound Dog."

He never caught a rabbit,
but she loved him anyway.
And she wept at the grave of
Elvis Presley.

The Shape of Jizz to Come

I come from the land of
Clark'dor.
The land of Bith.
From the ashes of
Lirin D'avi,
I picked up the
Kloo Horn
and road it to the far
reaches of the galaxy.
They were mad
about me.
I was mad about me.
I blew that Kloo Horn.
I saw the fall of
the bounty hunter,
that luckless Rodian.
Who shot first?
And a coin for a
bloody mess.

We came to the cantina,
we don't do weddings,
to rock the house.
We made those cowboys,
those scruffy looking
scum,
forget their fears
for a while.
We wailed
for a while.
I blew the Kloo Horn.
Many have shared
my stories.
Many have told my tales to

my tireless legion.

Ponda lost an arm
and poor Evazan lay dead.
I blew that Kloo Horn
and watched the
comings and goings
in that outpost of progress.
We traveled the stars
to see what could be seen.
A never-ending tour
and poor Evazon lay dead,
mad about no one.

Ishirō Honda to the Edge of Panic

It occurred to me
that we need a poem
about Godzilla.
It occurred to me that all
poems would be improved
by the inclusion of
Godzilla.

"Shall I compare thee
to a summer's day?
Thou art more lovely
and more Godzilla."

See?

"I celebrate myself
and sing myself
and what I assume
you shall assume
for every atom belonging
to me as good belongs to
Godzilla."

"Godzilla is the cruelest month."

On and on it goes.
Choose a poem from your
Intro to Poetry anthology.
Dial up a poem on
poetry.org.
Go to open mic poetry nights
or listen to slams in coffee houses.
Find a poem
that won't be improved by adding

Godzilla...
it can't be done.

"We real cool.
We skip school.
We a thrilla.
We Godzilla."

Over and over,
you can watch the movies,
read the comic books,
collect the vintage toys.
Over and over,
he makes the skies a little clearer
and the stars a little brighter.
Over and over,
nostalgia
and fear of the bomb
live in our souls.

"Once again, do I behold
Godzilla rolling
from his South Pacific island.
Once again, your heart beats faster
to see his name in verse."

"Whan that Godzilla
with his shouers soote."

The Modern Proboscis

Will the nose
of Una O'Connor
please stand up?
Present yourself
as you are.
A simple snout.
A great sniffer.
It sniffed the
Murry's Superior
on the scalp of
James Whale.
As she screamed
on the stair,
the pomade invaded
that stately shnozz.
As the transparent Rains
threw the bottle,
O'Connor's nose was
a perfect target.

The people's beak
scented out the
smoke of Flynn's
fashionable cigarette
as it wafted through
the room
on its way towards
the heavens.
Alone in the house,
O'Connor realized
none would know
the glory of her
honker.
As the green tights

and plumed hat
flew across the screen,
O'Connor's nose
was the perfect
emblem of the age.

Yub Nub, Motherfuckers

The 1983 *Sears Wish Book*
arrived before Thanksgiving,
and we poured over
those pages
afternoons after school.
Attempting to assist my parents,
I circled the items
I needed most:
Every item in
the entire toy section.
Castle Grayskull, The USS Flagg,
BA's sweet windowless black van
with the red stripe
and swivel seats for
Face and Murdock.
Always at the ready
with their rifles
and their improvisation,
Hannibal loved it when
a plan came
together.

I would have settled for
the Smurf Magic Talk Playset,
or Strawberry Shortcake's
Berry Bake Shoppe,
but the Star Wars section
was the section of true glory.
TIE-Fighters, X-Wings, Snow-Speeders,
the Jawa's Sandcrawler...
I wanted them all,
yet The Ewok Village Action Playset
was the real prize.
If only I'd been more specific

in my circling.
If only I'd been clear
with my parents.
If only I'd said,
"This is what I want.
Fuck all that other shit.
The Ewok Village
is my Holy Fucking Grail.
I want to live in the trees like
Wicket, Teebo,
and Logray.
I want to drop boulders on
Imperial AT-ST walkers.
I want to destroy the backdoor entrance
to the shield generator bunker.
I want to soar on a Sky-Glider
like Princess Kneesaa
to defeat the dreaded Gorax.
I want The Star Wars Ewok Village,
God damnit!"
Then, maybe,
just maybe,
those ancient youthful days
would have been as golden
as the Ewok's android God.
Then, maybe,
just maybe,
I could have raised my head
to the heavens
and shouted,
"Yub Nub, motherfuckers!
Yub Nub!"

Jumpsuit

The day I met Elvis Presley,
November 1975, has lived in
infamy as the day the storm
broke over Minnesota and
the *Edmund Fitzgerald*
came to rest on the floor
north of Whitefish Point.
I wore my greatest jumpsuit:
wide collar, white, sequined
breasts. The collar was wider
than the King's.
The white was whiter
than the King's.
The sequins shined brighter
than the King's.
He didn't like it.

No one should stand
head and shoulders
above him he thought.
The storm clouds crashed
and the lightning lit
the world. The white of my
jumpsuit pushed back those
flashes and blinded the King.
My sequined suit nearly
saved the freighter as she
broke up and nestled like
"an old man into a warm bath"
below the thunder.

Elvis wanted to shine brighter.
"You should show more
appreciation for my talents,"

he quipped, as he pointed his
Barretta at my chest.
I puffed it up to deflect the
bullet. Superior rolled on
and my jumpsuit shone
pure and bright.

Let the Rigatoni Be My Reeds

The ghost of John Coltrane
lives in my pantry.
He steals chickpeas,
long grain brown rice,
red lentils,
& black-eyed peas.
He comes out
once in a while
to stretch his translucent limbs
& rattle his transatlantic chains.

At night, I hear
Alabama, Lazy Bird,
Lulu Se Mama
float through the kitchen.
I'm laying in bed
and My Favorite Things
echoes off of a canister
of granulated sugar.
Sara asks me to
turn off the music
so she can sleep.
I say, "It's not me;
it's John.
He's up to his old tricks
again."
Haunted by a
sax player/
mad genius/
lover of licorice:
it could be worse.
Sometimes, during the day,
when he thinks no one is
watching,

he glides outside
to see the garden
and watches the progress
of the tomatoes and herbs.
Neighbors have whispered,
"Hey, I saw a creepy,
old guy in your
back yard yesterday."
"It's only Coltrane's ghost,"
I reply,
"checking the meter
and tapping his toes."

This is the year of the
semi-colon.
This is the year of the
everlasting jam.

When that tumor
consumed him,
only forty years old,
fans and critics
thought it was the end.
Loving wife
& loving kids
lowered him to eternal rest.
No rest for the wicked though.
He was live at Birdland,
live at the Vanguard.
He is live behind the pasta and marinara.

The ghost of John Coltrane
still searching for the
perfect al dente tone.

Quintero's Left Hook

We touched down
at Tampa International
& the swampy wall
caught us like
that old prize-fighter,
Manuel Quintero,
breaking his left hand
on Saguaro's right cheek.
We were down but not out
as we rented a truck
& high-tailed it to
Anna Maria.
In that unseasonably
sticky October,
we sweated through our clothes
& moved the furniture,
shoes, cooking utensils.
The house was empty
by the next morning.
The ref called time on Saguaro's face
& on what we've come to see as
our life on the island.
The house sold quickly
& we drove north
that same day with
all of Mable's trinkets,
trifles, riggings.
A catfish buffet in
South Georgia;
they served the same
at Circulo Cubana de Tampa.
Back on I-75 north
through the Smokies,
we pushed on across

the bluegrass of Kentucky
after midnight.
That U-Haul never went
as fast as when
she was barreling down
those mountain passes
& on across the great Ohio
double decker bridge.
She was fast as Quintero's
jaw-breaking jabs
& twice as deadly.
No one dared call that old girl
"Punchy;"
no one dared face down
Quintero
in the ring of the Cuban Club,
& that swampy wall of
Tampa-Bay humidity
took on all comers.

It's a Wonderful Life?

It's never rung true
for me.
I never understood
why people love it.

Now,
in my later years,
it's all become clear.
I figured out my problem
with the film.
It's predicated on the claim
that the world would is
better off
with George Bailey in it.

That's bullshit.
Our stuttering ass-hat
should put the movie
out of its misery
and just jump
already.

Martha Wayne's Pearl Necklace

In every version of her death,
1986 and onward,
we see the necklace split
and fall,
the pearls fly and crash.
They hit the darkness
through the empty chaos
and pain
his birth in the alley.
The image is impregnated
with empty symbolism;
Kane
and Finger confused.
Perhaps they signify
lost childhood and a poor little boy
disconnected,
in pieces, drowning.
Or maybe the pearls are capital.
Whitman's flag of green stuff
woven.
Joe Chill lets them lie.
Pearls that were his eyes,
child of oysters & banks
midtown
milky diamond district.
What did those men know
of loss… of death?
Miller
and Janson,
making it up
as they went along.

Loaves in the Rain

Like Ben Franklin
with his loaves
in the rain,
I carried my two
Seven Layer Burritos
across campus.
I sat in the hall
outside of the
classroom
and waited for
19th Century
American Lit
w/ Dr. Hauer.
Slowly, beautifully,
with care and precision,
I applied the Fire Sauce
and enjoyed
my ever-loving
lunch.

Two years later,
while the meningitis
ate his fast,
crazy brain,
he died in his bathtub.
I was in grad school,
a TA, then.
My supervisor found him
there, hunched over
in his bathroom.
Vomit on the floor.
We all got the news
at once.
At once,

I went and got two
Seven Layers Burritos.
With care and precision,
I applied the Fire Sauce
before I ate them
in his honor.

At the Dirt Mall
"Good buys, great people… earthy aroma."[1]

We hit the dirt mall
to avoid the fuckin'
mall cops
and find some
trinkets.
Grandma's birthday
was fast approaching,
so something
Grandma sized seemed
appropriate.

And the Dirt Mall
has it all

I bypassed the broken Walkman
from 1985
and the stack of old cassettes:
Journey's Greatest Hits,
Phil Collins – *Face Value*,
and an 8-track
Saturday Night Fever
soundtrack.
I saw the chipped Hummels
but kept on cruisin'.

And the Dirt Mall
has it all

There was Walt
with his stack of comics.
Never a bag or board
(the bloody savage),
never a book

I really wanted to read.
I read them none-the-less.
Endless X-Force, Omega Men,
Ri¢hie Ri¢h.
We talked about
the death of Superman
and whether The Thing's dork
is made of orange rock.

And the Dirt Mall
Has it all

I really hope Grandma
likes jumper cables,
Christopher Cross,
and back issues of *Sgt. Rock*,
because that's what she's getting
for her Big 8-0.
Everyone can use
jumper cables,
and if she doesn't like
the comic,
I suppose I can
always read it
while she gets caught
between the moon
and New York City.

1.   *Mallrats.* Written and directed by Kevin Smith, performance by
Jason Lee, Grammercy Picture, 1995.

Christ at the Comedy Store

On Sunset Boulevard,
the party never stopped.
No one slept;
no one took a cat nap
in the shadows.
No one nodded off
behind the dumpsters
in acerbic alleyways
behind the Garden of Allah.
Night clubs were packed
at all hours.
Into this scene strolled
the living Christ,
returning to save the souls
of the Strip.
He played The Whiskey,
The Roxy, The London Fog
into the wee hours of the night,
but at The Comedy Store,
He found his niche.
The crowd enjoyed
His new material,
comments on Gerald Ford
falling down and James L. Buckley
falling up.
Backstage, with Robin Williams
and Sam Kinison,
he performed new tricks.
His Miracle of the Baking Soda
kept everyone wired for hours.
He fed hundreds
with a single caquelon on fondue
and a glass of shrimp cocktail.
By 1982, Pauly Shore was
washing His feet with

those curly locks;
he was the weasel
through and through.
By the mid-80s,
His old standards
brought down the house.
Two thousand years ago,
the Beatitudes seemed
so earnest,
but now,
in the midst of Reaganomics,
they were just absurd,
and people rolled on the floor,
turning their other ass-cheek
over and over and over.
"The meek shall inherit
the Earth," He said.
It was hilarious.
Even Barabbas,
in the shadows at a back table
nursing a Rusty Nail,
chuckled a bit.
What's the deal with
peacemakers?" He asked.
They fell out of their seats.
Other nights, he opened with
the old stand-by
"Render unto Caesar."
Oh, how they howled
as they found their
tax loopholes.
"If you cast
the first stone…"
He said,
"…You might be a
redneck."

Wyatt Earp in Outer Space

Cracking skulls
in Dodge City, in Wichita,
on the great buffalo hunts,
Wyatt Earp had a dream.
While dealing cards
and pimping whores
in those back-water cow-towns,
Wyatt Earp had a dream.
He would lie in the tall grass
under the stars
of the Great Plains and wonder.
"How does one
make his fortune?" he asked.
"How can we strike gold
and make it count?"
He loved his brothers,
his family, his dentist,
but more so he loved his
money.
"Maybe we should mosey south;
we could book passage
and land in the land
of silver and the holy saguaro."
Wyatt Earp stared at those stars
and considered the moon.
The last great frontier.
"The moon could use a Marshall,"
the thought.
"The moon could use some
law and order."
Only getting there was the problem.

Virg had been a lawman
in California,

and he fought in the War
Between the States.
Virg had an idea.
Wyatt knew adventure
was out there,
even for a poor pimp with
bad teeth.

"Get some rope," said Virg.
And so Wyatt roped the moon.
He climbed and climbed
and climbed.
There are no saguaro
in the Sea of Tranquility.
There's no silver
in Montes Agricola.
But Wyatt found riches
of the mind.
He slept in the shadows of
Mons Esam,
a dreamless sleep:
contented,
at peace.

Guy in The Gobi

I had a dream last night.
In some odd reality show
exchange program,
Guy Fieri and Bear Grylls
traded jobs for a week.
Grylls was surviving
the dives of West Texas,
never suffering from thirst
as he chugged glass
after glass of ice water.
While listening
to *Tres Hombres*,
he had all the protein
he could ask for:
pulled pork sandwiches,
steak tacos,
Italian-Mex pizzas
w/ chorizo and
chihuahua cheese.

Conversely,
Guy was dying of thirst
in the Gobi Desert.
Scaling the Flaming Cliffs
and surviving on
the jellied eyes
of rotting Bactrian camels.
His head adorned
with his backwards Gatorz ,
he squeezed the fluid
from a ball of camel shit,
filtered it through is shirt,
and briefly quenched his thirst.
About 655,000 Americans die

each year from heart disease,
Guy tells us,
as he munches on rare
roasted racerunners.
While Fieri stuffed a few
filmy dome spiders
into his mouth,
he reiterated the
heart disease numbers
and wiped a tear
from his eye.
It was hard to keep
those tips so perfectly
frosted in
the Gobi Desert.

A Long Walk

"One equal temper of heroic hearts
Made weak by time and fate, but strong in will
To strive, to seek to find, and not to yield."[1]

Easter Sunday,
I walked three miles
to the record store.
It was cloudy and cold
in the spring of 1990.
The album had been out
since the previous Tuesday
and I needed it.
We'd waited as its release
was delayed
and delayed again.
I needed it.

At that store,
I'd bought NWA,
2 Live Crew, Ice T.
This was the only time
I was denied due to
the parental advisory
sticker.

I walked home
and convinced mom
to drive me back.
She gave permission
and I finally owned
Fear of a Black Planet.
How many records
have changed our lives?
How many records
created the blueprint
for our futures?

41

I was reborn that day.
Nevermore to rust
unburnished,
it was a long walk,
but I rose again
to seek a newer
world.

1.Tennyson, Alfred, Lord. "Ulysses." *Tennyson's Poetry*. Edited by Robert W. Hill, Jr. W.W. Norton and Company, 1999. P. 82.

Talking to Girls About Pirates

The first thing to do
when talking to girls about pirates
is to mention those shiny
gold doubloons
and pieces of eight.
They will probably enjoy your
Thurl Ravenscroft impression.
Girls always go for a nice
Ravenscroft.
It's a good idea to move on
to songs like "Yo Ho Ho
and a Bottle of Rum" or
"Yo Ho, Yo Ho a Pirate's Life for Me,"
but steer clear of Jimmy Buffet tunes;
a pirate can look at forty
all he wants,
but not if he wants girls to
look at him.

Once hooked,
it's time to reel her in.
This is when you drop
the Errol Flynn facts.
Since the dawn of man,
never has a girl been able to resist
Captain Blood.
For women may be
the death of us,
but this will be a very pleasant
way to die…
even if it is expensive.
Moving next to *The Sea Hawk*,
but then it's best to abandon Flynn
all together.

Maroon him in the Barracoons
and move on.

Robert Newton could
enchant women
at every turn.
He dragged his R's
and they dragged him to bed.
Once you've talked about pirates,
remember to talk
like a pirate
"Arrr, me lady,
hows about a cup of carrffee
and some barrrreakfast barrrritos?"
At this point, it might seem good
to offer Cap't Carrrrunch,
but that's just too obvious..

Before you mention Johnny Depp,
be sure to look in the mirror.
You never want to invoke
a better-looking dude
than the one she's talking to
at the moment.
Generally, stick to Yul Brynner
or Matthew Modine.
It's even best to avoid
Burt Lancaster.
Tim Curry's a risky one.
If she knows Cardinal Richelieu,
you probably don't need
to put forth this much effort.
If she prefers *Home Alone 2*,
you may in fact just
be screwed.

Once reeled in,
it may be time to drop anchor.
Be careful. Only the most
experienced pirate aficionados
successfully make the move
from conversation
to captain's quarters.
Parley and take your time.
The galley will egg you on,
but they are doubtless
really bad eggs,
Caution is a must.
If the pirates' life is in the cards,
a high wind will carry you home,
and you'll be swimming
in those gold doubloons
and pieces of eight.

All Good Things

In 1986 the world
mourned
the breakup of
Wham.
We had collectively
woken them up
before we went went.
Our whispers were careful
and exact.
Our deluge of tears
was constant
and true.

In 1999, our beloved
Baywatch abandoned
the sunny shores of
southern California
for the white sandy
beaches
of Hawai'i.
Our hearts were left
in Los Angeles.
The overhaul saw
the departure
of a cast who'd swam
into our living rooms,
swam into our hearts.
To the core,
we were
shook.

In 2015, we were collectively
rattled when Ren
ran his father through.

Han helped him do
what was needed.
We were all Chewbacca,
lashing out in anger
and sorrow.
What could ever break us
like the death of
General Solo?
Nothing could match
the pain.
Then, five years later,
in the fall of 2020,
the word went out.
Our lives would change
forever.
The flakey flour shell,
the melted cheese,
the sauce…
the Taco Bell
Mexican Pizza,
our one true
national dish,
was no
more.

I Definitely Dream In Color

But my film will be in
black and white
with lots of clowns
and contortionists
and legions of men with charcoal
umbrellas who wear
balmorals and cuff links,
saying things like
"Maybe not today" and
"Hurry up please, it's time" and
"You're a fine simple girl."

The Stuff to make
John Huston
proud.

Rainy and dark
like those late-night films
glowing through narrow
late-night windows
on late-night television sets,
after cigarettes and martinis
and masks
have vanished,
lost and forgotten.

The stuff
dreams are
made of.

The stuff to make
John Huston
proud.

Chuck Norris Action Jeans

His dresser drawer
filled with throwing stars,
nunchucks, a dull sai.
We donned Johnson's Baby Powder
to impersonate Paul Stanley,
Acc Frehley, Peter Chris.
We rocked and rolled all night,
and eyed his martial arts
accoutrements all day.

If only I too could have
suntetsu, emeici,
an amazing miaodao.
If only I too could be like
my cooler cousin.

He gave me one of his
many back-issues of
Black Belt Magazine.
I poured over those pages,
those advertisements
for weaponry my mother
would never let me get.

And then,
on the inside back cover,
it glowed.
It called to me.
She wouldn't be able to say "No."
Who could turn down
a request as simple
as this.
Unhemmed,
I could wear them "like regular

western jeans but with
the hidden gusset and stretch."
They wouldn't bind my legs
or rip out, and
with boys' sizes 6-20,
I knew I was ready.
A pair of Action Jeans to conquer
the world.

At the Grave of Little Sadie

Buried on a hill
in Thomasville,
Little Sadie
was all but forgotten
until Seven Foot John
dug her up
and rode her corpse
into the history books.
Blown down
in the streets of
Jericho,
her mother crying
and her baby alone,
Little Sarah Jones
never saw Bad Lee Brown
coming.
Little Sarah Jones
never saw her man
again.
Flowers laid out
and the church
songs sung,
she was lowered
to her shallow grave.
Covered with mud and rocks,
the grass grew
and the marker fell,
but Seven Foot John made us
remember.

And Bad Lee
became a hero.
We're to sympathize
with the mad gunman.

It became his
narrative.
The ballad of Lee Brown,
wild cat with a
hand cannon.
Holster under his bed.
But what of Little Sadie?
Forgotten suffragette
and waver of the flag
who spent years
on her back
for her momma
and her lonely baby.
Remember Little Sadie.
Visit the hill
in Thomasville.
Tip your hat and
bow your head
in memory
at the grave of
Little Sadie.

Our Garage, Our Dagobah

In the summer of '80,
we were adding a garage
to the side of our house.
It was a wide, two-car deal
with a fancy door
and a stairway leading
down to our basement.
A few years later,
I built a platform in the rafters,
carpeted it with samples
from a yard sale,
created a ladder up the studs
on the wailing western wall;
it was our sanctuary.
The early excavation
made mounds of dirt
which were perfect for
Star Wars toys.
We played in those piles
and Luke was once again
back on Dagobah.
He turned summersaults
and balanced the rocks,
crumbles of dirt really,
as we lost hours upon hours.
Luke carried Yoda
on his shoulders
as we carried our hopes
for the future in our hearts,
but Dagobah Luke was left out there
and is, presumably still, buried
in that foundation,
buried with those days.
Luke went the way of those hours,

he went the way of those hopes.
Later, on our raftered platform,
when we thought of
that back-yard Dagobah,
we thought of those innocent years
resisting the dark forces
of the galaxy.

Acknowledgements

Miyagi's Wisdom and the Lunch-Table Debates will appear in *The Daily Drunk* Summer 2022
Uber through the Sands of Akkaris appeared in *The Daily Drunk*, 28 October 2021
Ishirō Honda to the Edge of Panic appeared in *Sledgehammer*, 4 April 2021
Graceland appeared in *The Write Launch*, April 2021
Yub Nub, Mother Fuckers appeared in *A Thin Slice of Anxiety*, 28 February 2022
Jumpsuit appeared in *The Melbourne Culture Center*, April 2021
Let the Rigatoni be My Reeds appeared in *Tofu Ink*, Spring 2021
Martha Wayne's Pearl Necklace appeared in *Open Work*, 20 April 2021
Christ at the Comedy Store appeared in *Bombfire*, October 2021
Wyatt Earp in Outer Space appeared in *Muleskinner Journal*, 26 January 2022
Guy in the Gobi appeared in *The Daily Drunk*, 11 September 2021
At the Grave of Little Sadie appeared in *Cape Magazine*, 3 November 2021
Talking to Girls About Pirates will appear in *Alternate Route*, Summer 2022
Our Garage, Our Dagobah appeared in Riveting Rants

Andre F. Peltier (he/him) is a Pushcart Nominee and a Lecturer III at Eastern Michigan University where he teaches literature and writing. He lives in Ypsilanti, MI, with his wife and children. His poetry has recently appeared in various publications like CP Quarterly, Lothlorien Poetry Journal, Provenance Journal, Lavender and Lime Review, About Place, Novus Review, Fiery Scribe, and Fahmidan Journal, and most recently in Magpie Literary Journal, The Brazos Review, and Idle Ink. In his free time, he obsesses over soccer and comic books.

Twitter: @aandrefpeltier

Website: www.andrefpeltier.com

Made in the USA
Monee, IL
13 September 2022

12959052R00036